THEATER OF THE NEW

a collection of 100 progressive DVD theme projects, grouped in 10 sets of 10.

* * *

Change is the second most difficult thing;
Understanding, the first.

concept & design
by *Cliff Crego*

picture-poems.com/*dvds*

ON THE THEATER OF THE NEW—*Changing our perception of the world, one new idea, one new documentary, at a time*

This is a collection of some 400 films and documentary DVDs clustered around 100 progressive and topical theme projects. The theme projects are grouped in *10 sets of 10.* Working together with many friends, I've brought these films together over the past four years. Still very much a *work-in-progress,* it is designed both for individuals—young and old—to start their own viewing and discussion groups, or for self-study, or weekend theme workshops. This might happen at schools or universities, or in communities, both large and small. These film-viewing / discussion gatherings might be entirely casual, simply watching films now and then that for whatever reason strike one's fancy; Or they might constitute a more sustained and serious kind of enquiry, adding additional materials to selected films, discussing themes intensively in *dialogue groups,* and going through the list from beginning to end. Indeed, the basic intention is to scatter the themes and films like seeds in the wind. *How* and *where* and *why* they take root and perhaps flower will very much depend on the situation, and the needs, skills and experience of those involved. I can easily imagine a gifted yet isolated young artist with nothing but access to a laptop and the internet devoting his- or herself—entirely alone perhaps—to a kind of solo journey through the whole of the project. At the other extreme, I can also see before me a dialogue group—either virtual or working physically together—using the content of each film as a means to focus discussion and dialogue in a very much more general way.

Most of the films brought together, as a kind of Umberto

Eco-styled *infinite list,* are happily now readily available, sometimes streamed on-line for free or for a reasonable price, or at your Public Library, or as old-fashioned neighborhood rental DVDs.

The *why* of the THEATER OF THE NEW is very simple. Despite all the advances of communications technology, in my view, citizens of Western democracies, even though they enjoy the tremendous privilege of freedom of speech and expression—not one of the project's films would be possible without it—are tragically asleep at the wheel. It is as if all the violence and all the injustice of the world is taking place, so to speak, *off stage,* out of view. There are many reasons for this, some of which are explored in the featured films. The basic idea is to shift our focus to these "dark areas" which are to my way of thinking of great relevance for the future of humanity and the planet. My guiding principle is this: if the most basic crisis of our time is the crisis of perception, which I think it is, then what I demand of a film—regardless of *when* or *where* or *by whom* it was made—that it should make a difference in this regard.

I would say to one and all: *Have at it! Clean out your garage, borrow a beamer and hang up an old bed sheet! And get going!* Like Bertolt Brecht said: *"Change the world; it needs it."*

Start your own **THEATER OF THE NEW**, today!

View as webpage at:
http://picture-poems.com/dvds

Or download this booklet for free at:
http://picture-poems.com/dvds/theater-of-the-new_100-DVDs.pdf

If you need help setting up a group, or would like me to help conduct a dialogue group or workshop, or have suggestions for new films, email to cliff@picture-poems.com

Wild Ridgeline, the Eagle Cap Wilderness, Northeast Oregon

SET I: *war, water & waste*

(1) **Why We Fight** (Eugene Jarecki; 2005);

War Made Easy: *How Presidents & Pundits Keep Spinning Us To Death* (Norman Solomon / Media Education Foundation 2007);

Scarred Lands & Wounded Lives: *The Environmental Footprint of War* (Alice and Licoln Day 2008);

(2) **Battle's Poison Cloud**: *The 2,4-D / 2,4,5-T dioxin legacy of the American/Vietnam conflict* (Cecile Trijssenaar 2004)

Aftermath: *The Remnants of War* (Daniel Sekulich 2001);

Disarm: *Jody Williams & BAN* (Mary Wareham, Brian Liu 2005);

(3) **Blue Gold**: *The Fight to Stop the Corporate Theft of the World's Water* (Sam Bozzo 2009);

Flow: *For Love of Water* (Irena Salina 2008);

Thirst (Alan Snitow / Deborah Kaufman 2004)

(4) **Food, Inc.** (Eric Schlosser / Robert Kenner 2008);

The Future of Food (Deborah Koons Garcia 2004);

Fed Up! (Angelo Sacerdote 2002);

King Corn (Michael Pollan / Ian Cheney 2007);

Killer at Large: *Why Obesity is America's Greatest Threat* (Steven Greenstreet 2008)

(5) **The End of America** (2008 Naomi Wolf);

Der Untergang (Downfall: *Hitler and the End of the Third Reich)* (Oliver Hirschbiegel 2004);

Sophie Scholl: *Die letzen Tage* (**Sophie Scholl**: *The Final Days)* (Marc Rothermund 2005);

(6) **The End of Suburbia** (Gregory Greene 2004);

Escape from Suburbia (Gregory Greene 2007);

The Power of Community: *How Cuba survived Peak Oil* (Faith Morgan 2006);

Home (Ursula Meiers 2010)

(7) **Burning the Future**: *Coal in America* (David Novack 2008);

Energy Crossroads: *A Burning need to change course* (Christophe Fauchere 2008);

Coal Country (Phylis Geller 2009);

Harlan County, U.S.A. (Barbara Kopple 1976);

(9) **Crude Impact** (James Jandak Wood 2007);

A Crude Awakening: *The Oil Crash* (Basil Gelpke & Ray McCormack 2006);

Crude (Joe Berlinger 2009)

Oil On Ice (Bo Boudart / Dale Djerassi 2004);

(8) **Melting of the High Mountain Glaciers of the World**: *Abrupt Climate Change and our Future* (Dr. Lonnie Thompson 2007);

Extreme Ice (James Balog / PBS 2009)

Heat: *Frontline* (Martin Smith 2008);

(10) **Who Killed the Electric Car** (Chris Paine 2006);

Powershift: *energy + sustainability* (Kirk Bergstrom 2004);

Life With Principle: *Thoreau's Voice in Our Time*;

E2 Design: *Season 3* (Tad Fettig 2009);

Digital Nation (FRONTLINE / Rachel Dretzin 2010)

"The Island," confluence of Crooked & Deschutes Rivers, behind Round Butte Dam

SET II: *conquest & empire*

(11) **The Giant Buddhas** (Christian Frei 2005);

Obama's War: *Frontline* (Martin Smith / Marcela Gaviria 2009);

Hearts and Minds (Peter Davis 1974);

(12) **Ancient Futures**: *Learning from the Lahdak* (John Page / Helena Norberg-Hodge 1993);

Paradise, with Side Effects (Claus Schenk 2004);

Tibet: *Cry of the Snow Lion* (Tom Peosay 2003);

(13) **Lewis & Clark**—*Great Journey West* (National Geographic: Karen Goodman / Kirk Simon 1997);

Surviving Lewis & Clark: *The Nimiipuu Story* (Dan Kane, with Lewis & Clark College and the Nez Perce Tribe);

The Story of the Bitteroot: *A Cross-cultural Odyssey of Discovery* (1997)

(14) **War Photographer** (Christian Frei / James Nachtwey 2001);

Manufactured Landscapes (Photographs of Edward Burtynsky / Jennifer Baichwal 2006);

Light Keeps Me Company (Ljuset håller mig sällskap): (Sven Nykvis / Carl-Gustaf Nykvis 2000);

Henri Cartier-Bresson: *The Impassioned Eye* (Heinz Bütler 2003)

(15) **Triage**: *Dr James Orbinski's Humanitarian Dilemma* (Patrick Reed 2008)

Collaspe: (National Geographic / Jared Diamond 2010);

Hot Spots: *A journey to the world's most endangered areas* (Conservation International / Russell Mittermeier 2008)

(16) **Who's Counting**: *Marilyn Waring on Sex, Lies and Global Economics* (Terre Nash / The National Film Board of Canada 1996);

Guns, Germs and Steel (National Geographic / Jared Diamond 2005);

Conquistadors (Michael Wood 2000);

(17) **Bad Seed**: *The Truth About Our Food* (Jeffery Smith / Timo Nadudvari / Adam Curry 2006);

The Hidden Dangers in Kids' Meals: *Genetically Engineered Foods* (Jerremy M. Smith 2005);

Mad Cowboy Lecture (Howard Lyman 2005);

A Sense of Wonder (Kaiulani Lee / Christopher Monger 2010)

(18) **Reel Bad Arabs** (Dr. Jack Shaheen / Sut Jhally Media Education Foundation 2006);

Peace, Propaganda & the Promised Land (Media Education Foundation 2004);

No End in Sight (Charles Ferguson 2007);

Iraq' s Guns for Hire (National Geographic / Lisa Ling 2007)

(19) **Plunder:** *The Crime of Our Time* (Danny Slechter 2009);

The Ascent of Money: *The Financial History of the World* (Adrian Pennik 2008);

The End of Povery? (Phillipe Diaz 2007);

Casino Jack and the United States of Money (Alex Gibney 2010)

(20) **Viva Vivaldi! Cecilia Bartoli & Il Giardino Armonico**: *Arias and Concertos* (Paris 2000);

The Panama Deception: *Exposing the Cover Up!* (Barbara Trent / David Kasper 1992)

CUBA MIA: *Portrait of an All-Woman Orchestra* (Zenaida Romeu/Camerata Romeu / Cecilia Domeyko 2003)

Rocky Mountain Front, Montana, south of Glacier Nation Park . . .

SET III: *the future of humanity*

(21) **The Future of Humanity I & II:** *David Bohm & Jiddu Krishnamurti* (Mystic Fire Video 1985);

Light at the Edge of the World (Wade Davis 2008);

Tibetan Refugee (Dalai Lama, Robert Thurman, Yungchen Lhamo 2004);

(22) **The Corporation** (Mark Achbar / Jennifer Abbot 2004);

No Logo (Naomi Klein / Media Education Foundation 2003);

Let's Make Money (Erwin Wagenhofer 2009);

Gomorrah (Roberto Saviano / Matteo Garrone 2008);

(23) **With all Deliberate Speed**: *1954 Brown vs. Board of Education* (Peter Gilbert 2004);

Cases in Controversy: *The 14th Amendment* (Jumby Bay Studios 2003);

Unprecedented: *The 2000 Presidential Election* (Richard Ray Perez / Joan Sekler 2002);

United States Constitution (Goldhil Video 2004);

Invisible Ballots (William Gazecki 2005)

(24) **Wal-Mart**: *The High Cost of Low Price* (Robert Greenwald 2005);

Trashed: *"Trashing the earth . . .one day at a time"* (OXI productions 2007);

Story of Stuff (Annie Leonard 2007); **Story of Electronic Waste** (Annie Leonard 2010);

(25) **ENRON**: *The Smartest Guys in the Room* (Alex Gibney 2005);

The Money Masters (John Train 2008);

Brother, Can You Spare a Dime (Phillipe Mora 1975);

Money as Debt: *Animation by Paul Grignon* (2007);

The Warning: *Frontline* (Brooksley Born / Michael Kirk 2009)

(26) **Noam Chomsky:** *Crisis and Hope: Theirs and Ours* (2910)

Noam Chomsky: *Rebel Without a Pause* (Will Pascoe 2003);

Manufacturing Consent: *Noam Chomsky and the Media* (Peter Wintonick / Mark Achbar 1992);

ReGeneration (Phillip Montgomery 2010)

Outfoxed: *Rupert Murdoch's War on Journalism* (Robert Greenwald 2004);

(27) **Capitalism**: *A Love Story* (Michael Moore 2009)

Sicko (Michael Moore 2006);

FOODMATTERS (James Colquhoun /Laurentine ten Bosch 2009)

(28) **Climate Change**: *Coral Reefs on the Edge* (Hoegh-Guldberg 2009);

Six Degrees Could Change the World (National Geographic / Alec Baldwin 2007);

Nostradamus: *Prophet of Doom* (1995)

(29) **Ralph Nader:** *An Unreasonable Man* (Henriette Mantel Steve Skrovan 2006);

The War on Democracy (John Pilger 2007);

South of the Border (Oliver Stone 2009)

(30) **The Sketches of Frank Gehry** (Sydney Pollack 2005);

Aboriginal Architecture Living Architecture (Paul M. Richard 2005);

Transforning Energy (Chuck Davis 2006);

SET IV: *culture & nature*

(31) **Fire on the Mountain** (Beth & George Gage / First Run / Icarus Films 1995);

Monumental: *David Brower's Fight for Wild America* (Kelly Duane 2005);

Troubled Waters: *The Dilema of Dams* (Beth & George Gage 2003);

Discover Hetch Hetchy (Environmental Defense 2006);

(32) **Rethinking the Forests** (Oregon Public Broadcasting 2003);

A Silent Forest: narrated by David Suzuki (2007);

Civilian Conservation Corps (American Experience / 2009)

(33) **Methuselah Tree**: *Story of the Bristlecone Pine* (NOVA 2001);

American Indian Homelands: (Barry ZeVan 2006);

Homeland: *Four Portraits of Native Action* (Katahdin Foundation 2007):

(34) **Grizzly Man** (Werner Herzog 2005);

Staying Safe in Bear Country (International Association for Bear Research and Management 2001);

Examined Life (Astra Taylor 2008)

(35) **Anne Frank Remembered** (Jon Blair 1995);

Undergängens Arkitektur (**The Architecture of Doom**) (1991)

Im Toten Winkel: *Hilters Sekretärin* (**Blind Spot**: *Hitler's Secretary*) (Traudl Junge /André Heller & Othmar Schmiderer 2002);

The Anna Akhmatova File (Lichnoe delo Anny Akhmatovoy) (Semyon Aranovich 1989)

(36) **Ecological Design**: *Inventing the Future* (Brian Danitz 1994);

Buckminster Fuller: *Thinking Outloud* (Karen Goodman & Kirk Simon 1996);

Buckminster Fuller: *The Lost Interviews* (2005)

(37) **Dirt!** *The Moview* (Bill Benenson, Gene Rosow, Eleonore Dailly 2009);

Farming with Nature (Sepp Holzer / Permaculture in the Alps);

Aquaculture: Synergy of Land and Water (Sepp Holzer / Permaculture in the Alps);\

Global Gardner: *Permaculture with Bill Mollison* (Julian Russell & Tony Galley 1997);

The Close to Nature Garden (Masanobu Fukuoka / Margie Kamine 1982)

(38) **Earth Days**: *American Experience* (Robert Stone 2009)

Natural Connections (Bullfrog Films 2000);

Building Social Business Ventures / Banker for the Poor / Creating a Poverty-free World (Muhammed Yunus 2006);

China Blue (2008);

(39) **Hijacking Catastrophe**: *9/11, Fear, & the Selling of American Empire* (Jeremy Earp / Sut Jhally 2004);

Uncovered: *The War in Iraq* (Robert Greenwald / David O. Russell 2004);

Orwell Rolls in his Grave (Robert Kane Pappas 2004);

WMD: *Weapons of Mass Deception* (Danny Schechter 2004);

(40) **Gustav Mahler**: ***Conducting Mahler*** / *I Have Lost Touch With the World* (Frank Scheffer 2005);

Mahler Symphony No. 5: *Claudio Abbado, Lucerne Festival Orchestra* (2005);

J.S. Bach—***Johannes Passion***: *three performances*—Suzuki, Richter & Cloeberry;

Antigone (Geneviève Bujold / Gerald Freedman 1972)

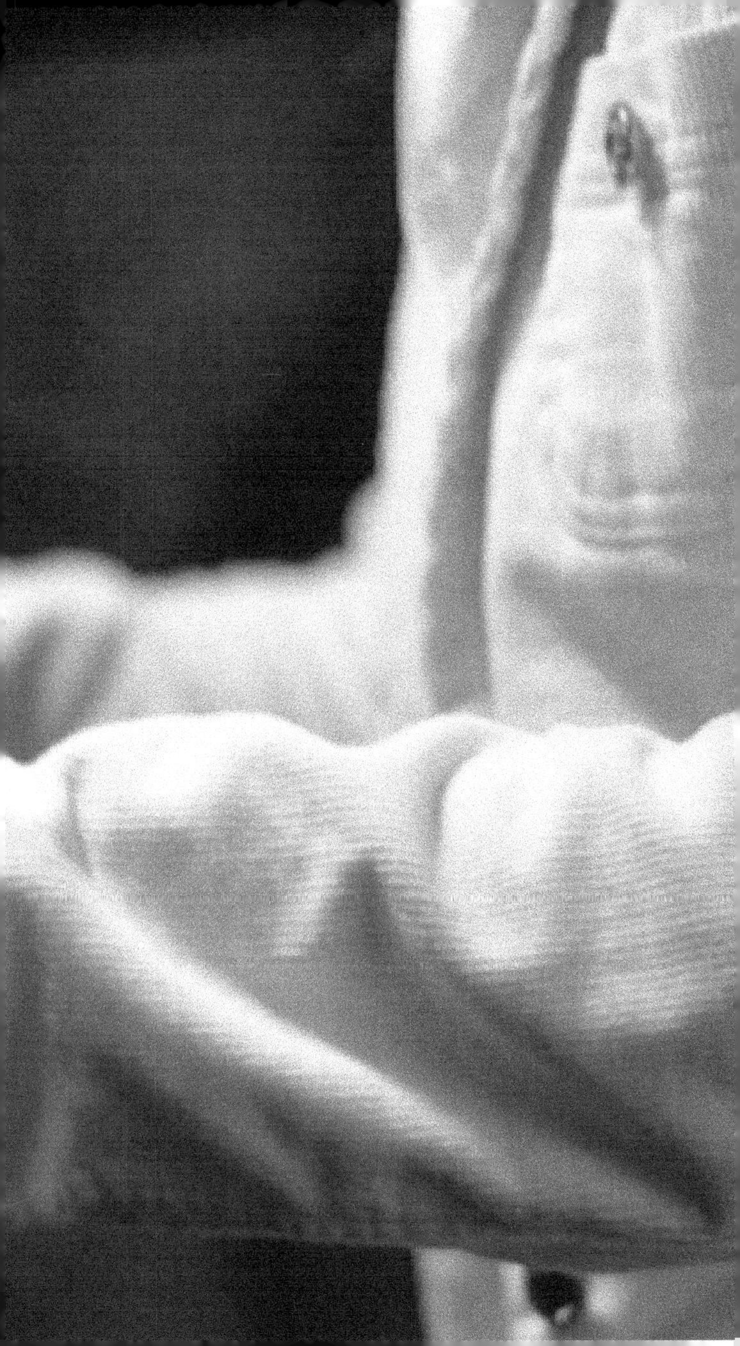

SET V: *generation of war*

(41) **Triumph des Willens (Triumph of the Will)** (Leni Riefenstahl 1934);

The Nazis: *A Warning from History* (BBC 1997);

Olympia I + II (Leni Riefenstahl 1936):

Great Conductors of the Third Reich: *Art in the Service of Evil* (1997);

Nietzsche and the Nazis (Stephen Hicks 2006)

The Great Dictator (Charlie Chaplin 1940)

(42) **Path to War** (John Frankenheimer 2002);

Winter Soldier (Winterfilm in association with *Vietnam Veterans Against the War* 1972);

Vietnam's Unseen War: *Pictures from the Other Side* (NGV 2002 War Photographer Time Page);

Inside the Vietnam War (National Geographic 2008)

(43) **America:** *Freedom to Fascism* (Aaron Russo 2006);

The Trials of Henry Kissinger (Eugene Jarecki; 2002);

The Most Dangerous Man in America: *Daniel Ellsberg and the Pentagon Papers* (Judith Ehrlich /Rick Goldsmith 2009):

(44) **All the President's Men** (Alan J. Pakula 1975);

Unconstitutional: *The War on Our Civil Liberties* (Nonny de la Pena 2004);

Lysistrata: *Women prevent war by withholding sexual favors from their husbands* (Aristophanes / Yiannis Negrepontis

(45) **Vietnam:** *The War at Home* (Glenn Gilber & Barry Alexander Brown 1979);

Berkeley in the Sixties (Mark Kitchell 1990);

One Bright Shining Moment (George McGovern / Stephen Vittoria 2005);

(46) **La Meglio Gioventù** (The Best of Youth 2003);

Heimat: *Chronicle of Germany* (Edgar Reitz 1984);

(47) **What Would Jesus Buy?** (Rev. Billy / Rob VanAlkemade 2007)

Jesus Camp (Heidi Ewing / Rachel Grady 2006);

Expelled: *No Intelligence Allowed* (Ben Stein / Nathan Frankowski 2008)

The Fire Next Time (Patrice O'Neil 2005);

(48) **The Glory of Spain**: *Music & Masterpieces from Madrid's El Prado Museum* (Andrés Segovia, Alicia de Larrocha, Victoria De Los Angeles 1967)

Guitarra!: *A Musical Journey Through Spain* (Julian Bream 2000);

Vincent: *The Life & Death of Vincent van Gogh* (John Hurt 1988);

(49) **The Peace** (Gabriele Zamparini / Lorenzo Meccoli 2003);

Bonhoeffer (Martin Doblmeier 2003);

A. Einstein: *How I see the world* (PBS: Richard Kroehling 1991);

Interview with David Bohm (Mystic Fire Video 1994);

Manda Bala (**Send a Bullet**) (Jason Kohn 2007);

(50) **Mahatma Gandhi**: Pilgrim of Peace (Biography 1997);

Gandhi (Richard Attenborough 1982);

The Making of the Mahatma (Shyam Benegal 1996);

Battle of the X-Planes: (Nova 2002)

CAUTIO
SHARP CURV
FALLING ROC
SEVERE SLID
NEXT 38 MIL

SET VI: *silent springs*

(51) **Rachel Carson's Silent Spring** (PBS 1993);

Heavy Metal (Northern Idaho's Silver Valley: Hans Rosenwinkel 2004);

Downwind Downstream: *Threats to the Mountains and Waters of the American West* (Christopher McLeod 1987);

The World According to Monsanto (2008);

Unser Täglich Brot (Our Daily Bread) (Nikolaus Geyrhalter 2005);

Historic Crop Dusting Films DVD: *1947 - 1969 Agricultural Pesticides,Insecticides, & Herbicides Films*; **Classic Pollution Films DVD**: *1930's - 1970's Water, Land & Air Pollution Films*

(52) **The Miracle Worker** (Arthur Penn 1964);

Unconquered: *Helen Keller in Her Story* (Nancy Hamilton 1955);

Blindsight (Lucy Walker 2006)

(53) **For All Mankind** (Natioinal Geographic Society 1989);

Apollo 13: *To the Edge and Back* (Noel Buckner / Rob Whittlesey 1994);

Apollo 13: (Ron Howard 1995);

To the Moon: NOVA (1999);

In The Shadow of the Moon (David Sington / Christopher Riley 2006)

(54) **Trinity and Beyond**: *Atomic Bomb Movie* (1995);

The Atomic Cafe (1982);

Nukes in Space: *The Rainbow Bombs* (Peter Kuran 1999);

Arming the Heavens: *The Push for Weapons in Space* (Glenn Baker 2004);

Building Bombs (*The Savannah River Plant* / Mark Mori / Susan Robinson / Jane Alexander 1990);

White Light, Black Rain: *The Destruction of Hiroshima and Nagasaki* (Steven Okazaki 2007)

(55) **Dr. Strangelove** (Stanley Kubrick 1964);

Thirteen Days (Roger Donaldson 2000);

Modern Marvels: *The Manhattan Project* (The History Channel 2002);

American Experience: *The Trials of J. Robert Oppenheimer* (David Grubin 2009);

Radio Bikini: *The most Terrifying and Unbelievable story of the Nuclear Age* (Robert Stone 1987)

Helen's War (Anna Broinowski 2004);

(56) **Slavery and the Making of America**: 1. *The Downward Spiral;* 2. *Liberty In the Air;* 3. *Seeds of Destruction;* 4. *The Challenge of Freedom* (WNET Dante J. James 2004);

The Devil Came on Horseback (Brian Steide 2007);

I Am Because We Are (Nathan Rissman 2008)

(57) **Killing Us Softly 3** (Jill Kilbourne 2000);

Born Into Brothels (Ross Kauffman / Zana Briski 2004);

Stolen Childhoods (Len Morris 2005);

(58) **Howard Zinn:** *You Can't Be Neutral on a Moving Train* (Deb Ellis 2004);

The People Speak: (Howard Zinn / Chris Moore 2009);

Instant Mix: *Imperial Democracy* and *Come September* (Arundati Roy 2008)

(59) **Ansel Adams**: *American Experience* (Ric Burns 2002);

Grand Canyon Adventure: *River at Risk* (Robert Redford 2008);

Drowned Out (Franny Armstrong / The River Narmada Dams Projects 2004);

River Ways (The Snake River / Colin Stryker 2007);

Swim for the River (Christopher Swain / Tom Weidinger 2006)

(60) **The Ecological Footprint:** *Accounting for a Small Planet* (Mathis Wackernagel / Patsy Northcutt 2005)

The Naturalist (Kent Bonar/ Doug Hawes-Davis 2001);

No Impact Man: *The Documentary* (Laura Gabbert / Justin Schein 2009);

Radically Simple (Jim Merkel / Jan Cannon 2005)

SET VII: *unknown worlds*

(61) **March of the Penguins** (Luc Jacquet 2005);

Encounters at the End of the World (Werner Herzog 2006);

The Endurance: *Shackleton's Legendary Antartic Expedition* (George Butler 2000);

Shackleton: *The Greatest Survival Story of All Time* (Charles Sturridge 2002);

The Last Place on Earth (1994);

90 Degrees South: *With Scott to the Antartic* (Alan Ravenscroft 1933)

(62) **Djabote**: ***DouDou N'Diaye Rose***: *Drummers of West Africa* (1991);

Tous les matin du monde (All the Mornings of the World) (Alain Corneau 1991);

Luciano Berio: *Voyage to Cythera* (Frank Scheffer 2005);

Fados (Carlos Saura 2007):

(63) **America's Lost Landscape**: *The Tallgrass Prairie* (David O'Shields 2005);

The Plow that broke the Plains (Pare Lorentz 1937); **The River** (Pare Lorentz); **The City** (Van Dyke, Copland 1939);

Surviving the Dust Bowl (PBS The American Experience; Chana Gazit 1998);

Climate Refugees (Michael P. Nash 2009)

(64) **Crapshoot**: *The Gamble with our Wastes* (Bullfrog Films 2003);

Homo Toxics (Carole Poliquin 2008);

Poisoned Waters (FRONTLINE 2009);

(65) **The Big Energy Gamble** (Arnold Schwarzenegger / NOVA 2009);

Human Footprint (National Geographic / Clive Maltby 2008);

The Future We Will Create: *Inside the World of TED* (Daphne Zuniga / Steven Latham 2007);

(66) **The Buddha:** *The Story of Siddharta* (David Grubin 2010);

Unmistaken Child (Nati Baratz 2008);

The Sun Behind the Clouds: Tibet's Struggle for Freedom (Ritu Sarin / Tenzing Sonam 2010)

(67) **Stravinsky** (Tony Palmer 1982);

The Rite of Spring (2-piano version 1990);

Stravinsky: *Le Sacre Du Printemps* (Pierre Boulez and the London Symphony Orchestra 1993);

(68) **Our Brand is Crisis** (Rachel Boynton 2005);
hiisurcoth

Cocalero (Evo Morales / Alejandro Landes 2007);

The Devil's Miner (Kief Davidson & Richard Ladkani 2005);

The Take: *Occupy, Resist, Produce* (Naomi Klein / Avi Lewis 2004);

The Charcoal People (Nigel Noble 1999)

(69) **The Fog of War**: *Eleven Lessons From the Life of Robert S. McNamara* (Errol Morris 2003);

Wir Sind das Volk (Protest of Silence) (Commemoration Concert of the Peaceful Revolution & Fall of the Berlin Wall 1999);

Live Concert from the Church of St. Nicolai, Leipzig: *Viktoria Mullova: J.S, Bach Chaconne;*

(70) **La Battaglia di Algeri (The Battle of Algiers)** (Gillo Pontecorvo 1965); *Edward Said Commentary;*

Diarios de motocicleta (The Motorcycle Diaries) (Walter Salles 2004);

Che Guevara: *Where You'd Never Imagine Him* (Manuel Perez 2004);

Fidel: *The Untold Story* (Estela Bravo 2002);

Sou Cuba / Ya Kuba (I Am Cuba) (Mikhail Kalatozov 1964)

Fireweed (Epilobium angustifolium), a beautiful circumpolar species

SET VIII: *world without coffee*

(71) **Black Gold**: *Wake Up and Smell the Coffee* (Tadesse Meskela / Nick & Marck Francis 2006);

Black Coffee: *A Glimpse into the Dark Side of the Brew* (Irene Angelico 2006);

The Coffee-Go-Round (Joost de Haas 2005);

A Walk to Beautiful: (Mary Olive Smith / Amy Bucher / NOVA 2007)

(72) **Control Room** (Jehane Noujaim 2004);

Iraq for Sale: *The War Profiteers* (Robert Greenwald 2006);

The Goebbels Experiment (Lutz Hachmeister 2005)

(73) **We Shall Remain** (American Experience 5-part series: 2009);

500 Nations (1995);

I Will Fight No More Forever (Richard T. Heffron 1975);

Arid Lands: *The Hanford Site & the Columbia Basin* (Grant Aaker & Josh Wallaert 2007)

(74) **Le Peuple Migrateur (Winged Migration)** (Jacques Perin, Jacues Perrin & Michel Debats 2001);

On the Wings of the Monarch (Leslie Ortabasi / Oktay Ortabasi (2001);

Global Warming: *The Signs and the Science* (Alanis Morissette / 2005)

(75) **Source to Sea**: *The Columbia River Swim* (Christopher Swain);

Jane Goodall: *Reason for Hope* (PBS 1999);

Unconquering the Last Frontier (Robert Lundahl 2002);

Building the Alaska Highway (2005)

(76) **Grappelli**: *A Life in the Century of Jazz* (BBC 2003);

Chet Baker: *Let's Get Lost* (Bruce Weber 1988)

(77) **Counting Sheep**: *Restoring the Sierra Nevada Bighorn* (Frank Green 2005);

Grass: *A Nation's Battle for Life* (Merian C. Cooper / Ernest B. Schoedsack 1925)

People of the Wind (Anthony Howarth 1976)

The Saltmen of Tibet (Ulrike Koch 1997);

Sweetgrass (Ilisa Barbash / Lucien Castaing-Taylor 2009)

(78) **Aristide and the Endless Revolution** (Nicolas Rossier 2005);

The Argonomist (Johnathan Demme 2004);

Haiti: *Killing a Dream* (Jonathan Demme / PBS 1992);

Life and Debt (Stephanie Black 2001);

(79) **Chartres Cathedral**: *A Sacred Geometry* (Keith Critchlow 2002):

J.S. Bach: *The Well Tempered Clavier* (BBC 2000);

Glenn Gould: *The Russian Journey* (1957);

Glenn Gould: J.S. Bach—*The Goldberg Variations*;

Chronik der Anna Magdalena Bach (Chronicle of Anna Magdalena Bach) (Jean-Marie Straub 1968);

(80) **Between Two Worlds: *Ravi Shankar*:** *In Portrait* (2002);

Etoiles: *Dancers of the Paris Opera Ballet* (Nils Tavernier 2001);

Stravinsky: *Les Noces* (Nijinska/The Royal Ballet 1996)

SET IX: *nature & meaning*

(81) **Bilby Brothers**: *The Men Who Killed the Easter Bunny* (Jim Stevens 2002);

Broken Rainbow (Maria Florio / Victoria Mudd 1985);

Rabbit-Proof Fence (Phillip Noyce 2002);

Echo Of Water Against Rocks: *Remembering Celilo Falls*

(82) **Djembefola**: *Mamady Keita;*

War Dance (Sean Fine / Andrea Nix 2006);

Sierra Leone's Refugee All Stars (Zach Niles / Banker White 2005)

(83) **Touch the Sound** (Thomas Riedelsheimer 2004):

Soundtrack for a Revolution (Bill Guttentag / Dan Sturman 2009)

Amandala! *A Revolution in Four Part Harmony* (Lee Hirsch 2002)

(84) **King**: *Man of Peace in a Time of War* (2006);

Dr. Martin Luther King, Jr.: *A Historical Perspective* (Thomas Friedman 1994);

Citizen King: *American Experience* (Orlando Bagwell 2004);

Freedom Riders: *American Experience* (Stanley Nelson / not yet released 2010)

(85) **Yellowstone:** *Battle for Life* (Peter Firth / Jeff Henry 2009);

Wolves in Paradise: *Ranchers & Wolves in the New West* (William Campbell 2007);

American Serengeti (National Geographic 2010)

(86) **MicroCosmos** (Claude Nuridsany / Marie Perennou 1996);

Genesis (Claude Nuridsany / Marie Perennou 2004);

Florilegium: *The Flowering of the Pacific* (Robert Hughes / botanist Joseph Banks /James Cook 1984);

Secret Life of Plants (Walon Green 1979)

(87) **The Linguists** (K. David Harrison, Gregory Anderson 2008);

Breaking the Maya Code (Michael Coe / David Lebrun 2008);

Die Frau Mit Den 5 Elefanten (The Woman with the 5 Elephants) (Vadim Jendreyko 2009)

(88) **Messner** (Les Guthman 2008);

The Dark Glow of the Mountains (Werner Herzog 1984);

Everest: IMAX (Ed Viesters, David Breashears, et al 1998);

Vertical Frontier (Kristi Denton Cohen with David Brower, Royal Robbins, Yvon Chouinard and Jim Bridwell 2002);

Am Limit (To The Limit) (El Capitan / Pepe Danquart 2007)

(89) **The Next Industrial Reolution**: *William McDonough, Michael Braungart and the Birth of Sustainable Economy* (Chris Bedford & Shelley Morhaim 2001);

I.M. Pei: *First Person Singular* (Peter Rosen 1997);

Museum on the Mountain (I.M.Pei / Peter Rosen 1998);

Visions of Italy: *The Grand Tour from a Stunning Aerial View* (PBS 2001/2002);

(90) **Beethoven: *Erocia***: *The Day that Changed Music Forever* (BBC / Nick Dear / John Eliot Gardiner / Orchestre Révolutionnaire et Romantique 2003);

Keeping Score: *Beethoven's Eroica* (Michael Tilson Thomas / San Francisco Symphony Orchestra 2006);

In Search of Beethoven (Phil Grabsky 2009)

DEA

WILL

DESTR

SET X: *ethics without religion*

(91) **Wheel of Time** (Wener Hezog 2003);

Clouds are not Spheres: *The Life and Work of a Maverick Mathematician* (Nigel Lesmoir-Gordon 2000);

Fractals: *Hunting the Hidden Dimesnion* (NOVA 2008);

Is God a Number?: *Maths that Mimic the Mind* (Sir Roger Penrose et al.);

(92) **The 11th Hour**: *Turn Mankind's Darkest Hour into its Finest* (Leonardo DiCaprio 2007);

Strange Days on Planet Earth 1 & 2: *Invaders; One Degree Factor; Predators; Troubled Water; Dangerous Catch; Dirty Secrets* (Edward Norton / National Geographic 2005 - 08);

Blue Vinyl (Daniel B. Gold & Judith Hefland 2002);

(93) **The Man Who Planted Trees** (Jean Giono / Frederic Back 1987);

Falkens öga (Kestrel's Eye) (Mikael Kristersson1998);

Ants: *Little Creatures Who Run the World* (NOVA Edward O. Wilson 1995);
Housefly: An Everyday Monster (1994);

Bees: *Tales from the Hive* (NOVA 2000);

Nature: *Silence of the Bees* (2008)

(94) **The Botany of Desire**: (Michael Pollan / Michael Schwarz 2009);

How to Save the World: *BioDynamic Farming in India* (Tom and Barbara Burstyn);

Food Beware: *The French Organic Revolution* (Jean-Paul Jaud 2008);

Wie man sein Leben kocht (How to Cook Your Life) (Edward Espe / Doris Dörrie 2007);

(95) **Mount St. Helens:** *Back from the Dead* (Nova 2010)

Deadly Ascent (NOVA / Denali 2006);

Touching the Void (Kevin MacDonald 2003);

Nordwand (North Face) (Philipp Stölzl 2008)

(96) **When the Levees Broke**: *A Requiem in Four Acts* (Spike Lee 2006);

Extreme Engineering: *Holland's Barriers to the Sea* (2004);

Hurricane on the Bayou (Meryl Streep / Greg MacGillivray 2006);

Detroit: *Ruin of a City* (Michael Chanan & George Steinmetz 2005);

(97) **Plan Colombia**: *Cashing in on the Drug War Failure* (Edward Asner 2002);

Speaking Freely: *Vol.4: Chalmers Johnson* (2007);
Speaking Freely: *Vol. 2: Susan George* (2007);
Speaking Freely: *Vol. 1 John Perkins* (2007);

Drug Wars: *parts I - IV* (2005)

(98) **The World's Most Dangerous Drug National Geographic:** (National Geographic / Lisa Ling 2006);

Hemp Revolution (Anthony Clarke 1995);

The Union: *The Business Behind Getting High* (Brett Harvey 2007)

(99) **Everything's Cool**: (Daniel B. Gold / Judith Helfand 2007)

Earth Report: *State of the Planet 2009* (National Geographic 2009);

World in the Balance: *The Population Paradox* (NOVA 2004);

(100) **The Cove** (The Rising) (Louie Psihoyos 2009);

Ethics and the World Crisis: *A Dialogue with the Dalai Lama* (2004);

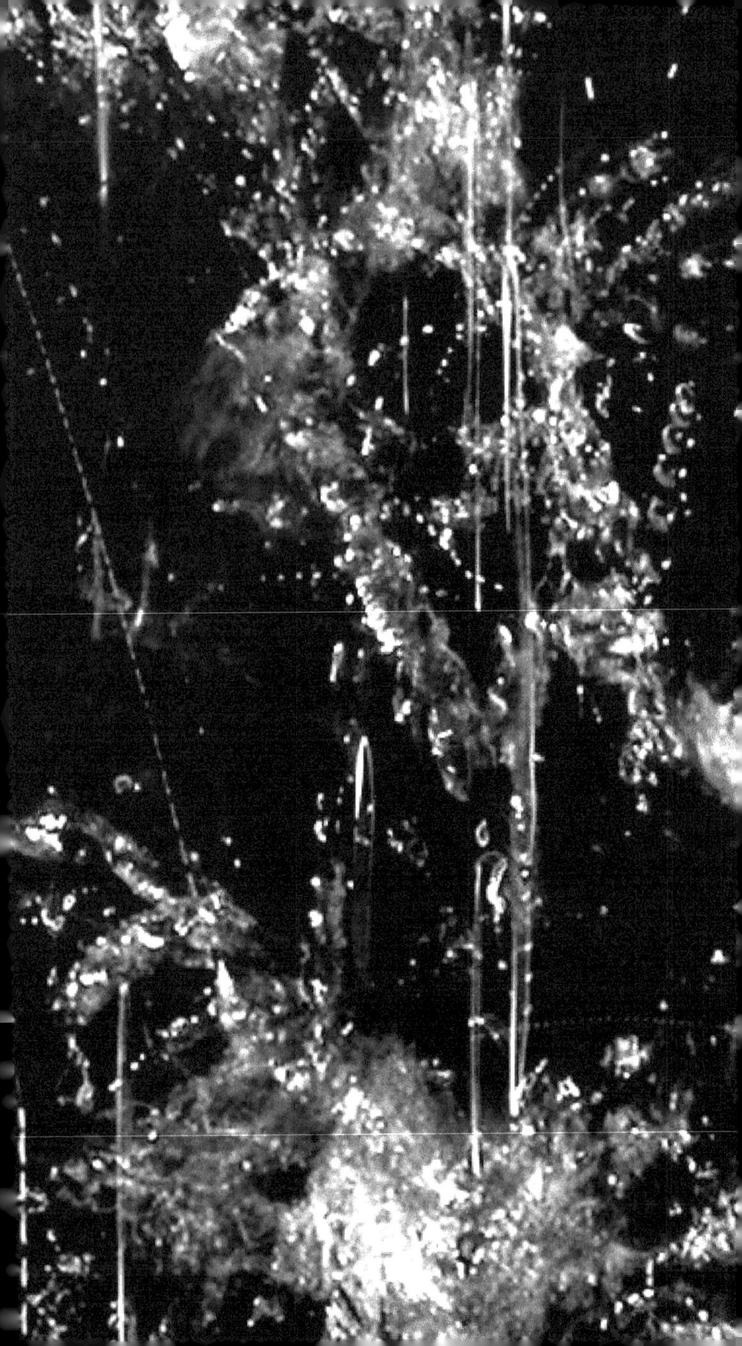

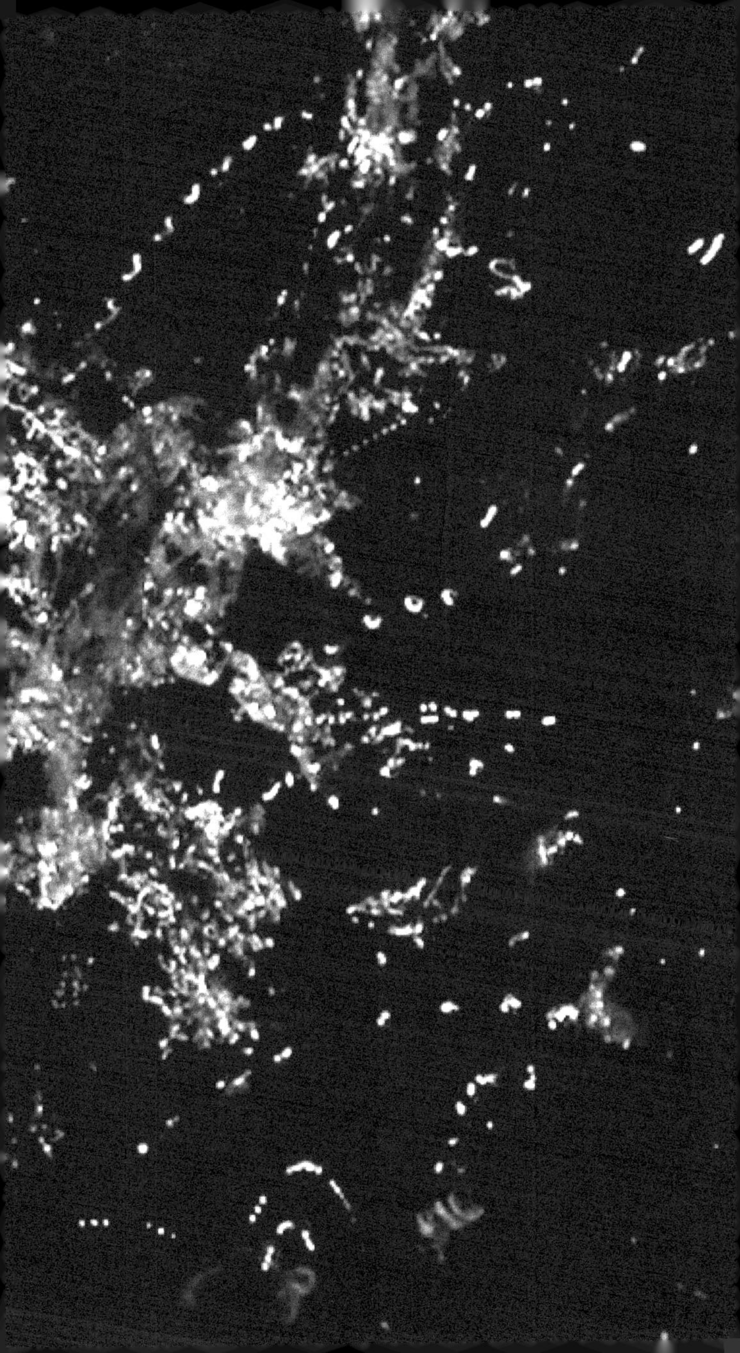

THE LIBERATION TRIANGLE—*a meditation on cultural change*

I've always felt that the simplest and most powerful of all possible tests is the test of doing without. It is simple because there is nothing new to buy, no new set of skills one must master, no lessons to attend. We simply stop doing something that we're used to doing. And it is powerful because we quickly become aware of how habit shapes perception. After all, it is possible that what we once thought was absolutely necessary and essential may turn out to be largely arbitrary, and, in a deeply insidious and unconscious way, destructive.

So, here are three key *do's* of present Western culture I've turned into a trio of *don'ts:*

The Liberation Triangle

don't drive

don't eat junk food

don't watch TV

There are other sets of three, of course. Perhaps some readers might come up with better collections themselves. It must be said that they are simple only in principle. To actually live them would be difficult. But also, I think, revealing. That is why I call the set of three *The Liberty* or *Liberation Triangle.* By just doing *one* of the three, we step outside of the dominant stream of everyday behavior. This is rather like venturing up to clearer, higher ground and looking down on the whole of a culture's activity in certain areas and directions. From the new perspective, suddenly we see pattern, we see motivations, and we see consequences and inter-relationships. And, we are surprised because the new vantage point makes these seem so obvious.

The Triangle can also be reversed. Interestingly, if we introduce just one of its three sides into a culture which hitherto has remained unexposed, we might conjecture that the integrity of that culture will quickly fall apart. This, it seems to me, suggests that the petrochemical cult of cars, the mesmerizing propaganda blitz of TV, together with the highly habit- forming nature of industrial agriculture's junk food, make for a kind of powerful mutually reinforcing illusion. A kind of perceptual prison, you might say.

Hence, the idea of liberation, of freeing oneself, by doing nothing more than *not* doing three key thing: *don't drive; don't watch TV; don't eat junk food.*

ON THE TRIANGLE OF RELATIONSHIP

The strength of the *triangle of relationship,* it seems to me, is that it in a gentle yet forceful way lifts us out of the isolation of the linear, fragmentary style of thinking which is so characteristic of Western thought. The basic idea is that, for every thought, every action, and every resource or artifact, there are always at least three sides, or three questions we must ask: *How is this thought or object related to myself; How is it related to others (society or culture)? And how is it related to the Earth, or the wider context?* Here's a rough sketch:

The key point is that these relationships co-exist in a movement of relational resonance which, although they are normally implicit and largely invisible, are at the same time, regardless of how we think about them or act towards them, indivisible. That is, when we pick up an isolated object, we are in actual fact picking up this triangle of relationship. We can easily imagine this in a visual way, say, like taking an apple and mapping out the normally unseen relationships not just to my own body as I eat the apple, but also to those who grew it, delivered it to the store where I bought it, as well as perhaps the actual place—the orchard—where it was grown. We might also imagine the triangle in terms of sound, as for example a singing voice in a large reverberant structure like a concert hall or cathedral. We have the sound of the voice as it appears to the singer him- or herself, but also the sound of the voice as it appears to others who listen to it in the same space. And, of course, there is the acoustic space itself, the wider context of what for the singer is the whole world, both literally and in the ritual sense.

Thus, we move naturally and easily from the top of the triangle, *me,* to others, *we,* and to the world or Earth, *all,* and back again. Notice also that this movement occurs both one-at-a-time (like musical melody), and all-at-once (like musical chords), a feature which is very unlike visual mirrors, but distinctive and natural to relational resonance as a whole.

With this sonic image in mind, it is easy to see the distortional nature of isolation and fragmentation. Think for a moment of the same singer, but now in a space completely devoid of resonance. Musicians find such spaces deeply disturbing. *"There's no echo!"* they say. They call such spaces 'dry' or 'dead.' In other words, the room or hall gives nothing back to them. So, it comes as no surprise that, without the natural sustaining resonance of echo, which both gives energy to the sound and makes it possible to blend and tune with oneself and others, we very quickly wish to stop singing altogether.

Now, if we go one step further and generalize this movement of resonance and think not just of sound but also relationship in terms of meaning and responsibility, we have, I think, the beginnings of a strong model of ethical awareness. Here we have the image not of sound, but of a woven fabric. I pick up a strand or thread—any thread, it makes no difference—and simply follow it to its source. This naturally reveals others connected to the same thread, as well as how the thread is woven into the fabric of the larger whole. Take coffee, for instance. In isolation, coffee is just a savory, pleasant, habit-forming stimulant for which we as users naturally wish to pay the best possible price for the best quality. But if we begin thinking about coffee with the relationship triangle in mind, a far richer story is revealed as we follow the highlighted thread of a single pack. It leads us to those who market, distribute, process the coffee, and most especially, those who actually grow and harvest the beans. Ultimately, we are led to the wider earth-bound ecological context which sustains both the growers and the coffee plants themselves.

If we follow this path of relationship, notice first that there is in principle no real fundamental difference between the ethical and environmental dimensions of awareness. They are but two inseparable aspects of the same movement, one which emphasizes *responsibility,* and the other which emphasizes *understanding.* Second, notice that in the current era, coming as we all do, including myself, from a state of radical isolation and fragmentation, the more consistently and energetically we pursue the thread, regardless of where it leads us, we are unavoidably going to be in for some shocks and highly disturbing information. The sweat shops and child labor behind my favorite running shoes; the half-lives of all the toxins found in their soles. The flame retardants in the laptop I love and depend on turning up in the breast milk of young mothers in the far Arctic North; or a kid in India, or China, or Africa, working barefoot atop a mountain of electronic waste, eking out a living by stripping away the equally toxic metals of the same computer once I'm forced to throw it away. Or, coming back to our first example, the coffee farmer in the high-country of Ethiopia who explains that he gets only 3 cents for each kilo of green beans he produces, and looks straight into the lens of the camera as he tells us that he needs at least 8 or 10 cents just to survive.

So one sees that the beauty and the strength of the triangle of relationship, just as with the musician with whom we began in the natural world of relational resonance, is that—like it or not—both harmony and disharmony are necessarily revealed.

Both the good and the bad. One can't have one without the other. This is a fact. And perhaps this is why the ethical awareness of the compassionate mind has evolved out of the inherently self-destructive isolation of the brutish brain. Where does this intelligence come from? Simply our genetic structure? Or from some much deeper and more subtle source? As with all really fundamental questions of existence, we find, I think, as we follow the triangle of relationship far enough that we are led to a point where we can only say with the honesty a small child demands, *"I don't know."* For here the known world ends, and the uncharted land of the spiritual wilderness of the extraordinary human mind begins.

ON THE NECESSARY SEPARATION OF ETHICS & RELIGION

One of the great fundamental insights of the U.S. Constitution, derived from the traditions of ancient Roman law, is the idea of balance of power. Of equal importance is the principle of the separation of religion and state. Now, it seems to me, that we would benefit greatly if we were to in a similar spirit of balance and clear structure *separate religion from ethics.* Indeed, I would argue that a new set of demanding moral problems makes such a division imperative.

Why? Because, in the view being roughly outlined here, the theater of moral debate demands that we check our cloak of sectarian beliefs at the door. For with moral questions, just as in a republic no one may claim to be above the law, in democratic dialogue, no one or no argument may make claims to absolute authority.

How then are we to decide what is good, right and just? Well, I would say by placing calmly the arguments, the evidence, or the competing theories on either side of the scales of truth. And then weighing their relative strengths and weaknesses within the widest contexts deemed relevant. For if we really consider this process carefully, what is of crucial importance—indeed, sacred, some would say—is the motionless, neutral center upon which the fair, unbiased balance of the scale depends.

[Whitebark Pine Snag (Pinus albicaulis) A keystone species under threat. Will it be granted Endangered Species status?]

ON THE DIFFERENCE BETWEEN *THE BRUTISH BRAIN & THE COMPASSIONATE MIND*

"You're either with us, or against us."
versus
"Whatsoever you do unto the least among you,
you do unto me."

This is what I see as one of the signature divides of our time, between the *brutish brain* and the *compassionate mind,* two defining features of our species that are now profoundly at odds with each other.

On the one hand, we have the brutish brain, which embodies the deep and rich legacy of the human animal's natural history, and has clearly evolved to meet and master the many demands of survival. It is not at all that different, it seems to me, from the brain of a wolf, or a bear, or an ape. The powerful engine of the brutish brain is the mechanical intellect of problem solving. How to make a better stick for digging roots, a better skin for carrying water, a sharper stone for a more deadly weapon. Its means is force. Its ethics is essentially the ethics of *the me, my* group, *my* nation. The identification of this smaller me with the larger group, which is then radically divided from the wider environment, is a key feature of the brutish brain. *What's good for me and my group is good; what's good for my enemies is bad.*

On the other hand, we have the evidently uniquely human compassionate mind. The compassionate mind sees itself in the other, sees itself mirrored everywhere in the world around it, and, like an infinitely large grandpiano, its strings seem to resonate and reflect all the other sounds of the symphony of life played around it. The energy of the compassionate mind is not just the problem-solving, computer-like ability of mechanical intellect, but rather intelligence. Intelligence is in this view a vastly more subtle movement of consciousness; it is this energy of intelligence which is evidently very much broader in scope and source than the isolated individual self. Its means or method is *understanding.* Its ethics is that of *the good of the whole,* the good of the widest context of which it is aware.

Now, remarkably, I think we could say that the human brutish brain, if it is not limited in some way and simply left to run off on its own, is potentially the single most destructive creation of evolution. At the same time, the compassionate mind, as far as we can know, is evolution's most creative achievement. The problem, of course, is that we in a confused way embody both. Clearly, the mind of compassion has come into being in part to limit the over the millennia ever-increasing lethal capabilities of the brutish brain, through understanding and insight, like a patient, loving mother checks the wayward tendencies of an overly aggressive, self-centered child.

We are now at a kind of tipping point, or threshold, concerning the relationship of these two, either conflicting or complementary, movements of consciousness. By this I mean a point beyond which it will become increasingly difficult to change course. The fundamental question is, down which path will we go, down which path will the energy of the world, of humanity, be led? Clearly, the brutish brain at present has tremendous mechanical power behind it. Its instruments are the corporate and military-industrial complex, and the financial and legal systems that have co-evolved to support, profit from, and protect these. Government at present, call it what you will—oligarchy, democracy, tyranny—serves overwhelmingly to safeguard these corporate and military interests.That is my view, and I stand by it. At the same time, the more enlightened democracies worldwide embody in a tragic way the very contradictory division of consciousness which is our theme. Freedom and civil rights are guaranteed. But only insofar as these do not get in the way of the more primary corporate and military interests.

This is why even potentially good leaders will be torn apart by present systems of government. Because the worst half, so to speak, will be forced to dominate. So leaders promise peace, but give us more war. They promise universal health care, but sell out to the insurance companies. They promise to address climate change, but give us more coal-fired and nuclear power plants. It is in a word why politics is at present the very worst place to look for leadership. Unquestionably, the way of the brutish brain, if it should for whatever reason be allowed to prevail, will lead to its ultimate apotheosis of total self-destruction. This is self-evidently so, especially when considered over longer spans of cultural time like two or three centuries, because of the already realized destructive potential of its weaponry, or simply because of the rapacious waste of resources and resulting damage to the biosphere inherent not only in their possible use but solely in their development. But the way of the compassionate mind, even though its voice is at present weak in the political arena, *has the power of necessity behind it.* And that makes all the difference. That is, if we see the difference with clarity, and with the energy of our whole being.

PATH OF VIOLENCE / PATH OF PEACE

The first mistake we make in dealing with the violence of the world is to name it evil. To name violence "evil," instead of simply calling it mistaken or bad, is to give violence the status of something like an independent "force of darkness" which is somehow actively out to do us harm. All beings, all systems, indeed, all materials and machines, have inherent points of| weakness between elements that may break down, that become subject to illness, or are otherwise easily corrupted. *Iron rusts; trees rot; people lose their humanity.* But this does not mean that some sinister autonomous power seeks to prevail, but rather that, for whatever reason, the goodness or wholeness of integrity has fallen apart. *The second mistake* in dealing with the violence of the world, made possible by the first, is to see this violence as somehow outside of ourselves, as somehow separate from our own essential nature, and therefore something to be fought against with the very same use of force we feel threatened by in the first place. Finally, *the third mistake,* made possible by the first two, is to believe that the resulting path of violence is somehow inevitable, and that we must therefore prepare for it by doing whatever is necessary in order to dominate when force becomes necessary, as we believe it most certainly shall. In this way, the preparations to defend ourselves against violence become—as a kind of *perpetuum mobile*—a primary cause of violence itself.

ON NECESSITY

The perception of necessity is liberating, because the way is then made free for clear, decisive action. Indeed, how could this be otherwise? When something *must* be so, the mind—whether that of the individual, or that of the collective—quits fighting against itself and wasting energy, and thereby, without forcing, comes to a unitary vision or flow.

ON THE DIFFERENCE BETWEEN *LIMIT & CONTROL*

Control imposes order *from without* by projecting the predetermined thought, conditioned by the past, of what *should* happen. The need to control invariably increases as the disorderly, unexpected, side-effects of past efforts accumulate, which results in ever-greater unnecessary difficulties or complicatedness. In contrast, *limit* allows order to emerge *from within* by determining only what at any given moment *should not* happen. Limit is therefore open to the future, and tends strongly towards ever-greater simplicity and freedom.

ON SUSTAINABILITY

(0) Sustainability is movement *without contradiction, without conflict, without waste;*

(1) Sustainability *is* Network *is* Community *is* Friendship;

(2) Sustainability is when natural law and cultural convention fit together like the shape of a well-crafted violin fits the laws of acoustics, of its spruce and maple woods, as well as the physical movements of the performer. Sustainability is therefore a state of dynamic, creative, and sometimes even generative chaotic, harmony;

(3) Sustainability is when the structures and norms of cultural convention adapt continuously to the exigencies of natural limit; Limit gives rise to the formative context; Art happens when the artifact reflects this formative context on all its sides, in all its myriad details.

(4) Sustainability is what we become aware of with the dire shortages of crisis; Contradiction is what we become aware of in the sudden surprise of total collapse; Freedom is what we become aware of when the Inquisitor knocks at the door.

CIRCULAR DECEPTION

We shape the world and the world shapes us.

In an ironic twist of meaning, present Western culture, which is arguably the most fragmented, a-rhythmic, and linear of all historical world societies, now uses an "it's cyclical" argument to explain away most every crisis thrown at it. The collapse of the economy? *"It's cyclical."* The collapse of icefields? *"It's cyclical."* Climate change, species extinction or, indeed, perhaps the collapse of the entire biosphere? *"It's cyclical!"* This reply is repeated over and over again like an old-fashioned vinyl record stuck in a scratchy groove. On the surface, the idea is that something has happened before, and now it is just happening again. Therefore, what's the problem? But deeper, the cyclical reply is really a thinly-veiled deceptive cover, an excuse so that we may in good conscience continue our remarkably non-cyclical straight-line lifestyle of destruction indefinitely into the future. Meanwhile, evidence to the contrary—of human-caused, profound and catastrophic disruptions of countless natural cycles—piles up around us like so many broken beer bottles and stray dogs in towns filled with people too drunk to care, or who are about to move someplace else.

Let's hope for the best.

TEXTURE OF THE WORLD—

on the watercourse way

The way of force and outward mechanical power
always run in a straight line.

For it, the way of water and the meadow meander
is just a waste of time.

NATURAL STRENGTH?

2 points, a *stick;*
3 points, a *system.*

UNLEARNING THE OLD

We shape the world and the world shapes us.

Learning the new is simpler than unlearning the old. To learn the right things, at the right time, and in the right way, is the intention which naturally not only takes its seat at the head of the class; it may be compelled to leave the school altogether for the freedom of the open field.

RHYTHM & TEMPO

Rhythm comes from walking;
Tempo comes from the heartbeat.

CONCLUSIONS & QUESTIONS

Conclusions fight;
Questions ask.

WASTE OF GOOD

We shape the world and the world shapes us.

Good people do bad things when forced to think and move within inherently false and contradictory systems.

The task of philosophy is to, without forcing, pause the disharmonious movement, and then step back to reconsider the inconsistencies, possible wrong turns, mistakes of direction.

WAR ON WASTE

The Earth supplies enough for all our wants and needs, but not for all our wars and waste.

TRINITY TEST— *July 16th 1945*

"Now I am become Death, the destroyer of worlds."
Robert Oppenheimer

ETHICAL IMPERATIVES—*a meditation on Earthrise*

The first imperative of ethics, it seems to me, is that ethics itself should not be thought of as belonging primarily to what is now considered religion, but rather as a primary dimension of *all* human activity. 'Primary' means here that it is simply the *first* aspect to be considered in all action and decision making, and *not the last.*

All action resonates in space and time. Sometimes only a second or two, sometimes for centuries; Sometimes only a few centimeters out from my own body. Sometimes perhaps to infinity.

Outwardly, this is *ethical consequence;* inwardly, itt is *ethical conscience.*

The key feature of this complementary inner and outer movement of consequence and conscience is the breadth of the circle of awareness and responsibility. The great leap of consciousness brought home in the historic *Apollo 8 Earthrise* photograph made by astronaut William Anders in 1968—perhaps the most important image of our time—is that it shows to the mind of compassion with granite-like clarity that the necessary breadth of this circle of awareness and responsibility begins and ends with the whole of the living Earth, and not with largely arbitrary, conflicting fragments, like current nations states.

Necessity is a thing of great philosophic beauty. This is so because necessity awakens, and in a most powerful way brings together, the very best of our intellectual and spiritual energies, both individually and collectively. Just as the wild proposal of the poet-politician that we must go to the Moon not because it is easy, but because it is difficult, crystallized and brought together an entire generation of creativity, we need now to see that the dual imperatives of the new millennium are *ending waste and war. Waste,* because it in one word summarizes where the *conventions of Culture* are out of step with the *laws of Nature.* Eliminate waste, and you solve the problems of

[Historic *Earthrise* photo by William Anders, Apollo 8 mission]

pollution, renewable energy, corrupt agricultural practices and climate change all at once. *And War,* because of its destructive insanity—and *it is* insanity because the entire Earth is now at stake—of contemporary weapons technology stands before us as the central fact of our time:—that it is *no longer a question of violence or non-violence,* as Dr. King suggested also about forty years ago, *but rather of non-violence or non-existence.* Seen from this larger perspective, it becomes clear perhaps that War and Waste are essentially two sides of but one problem.

For who would not say that, from the perspective of the Moon, waste is indeed humanity's *total war on Nature?* And that, in turn, war is not humanity's total waste of its own spiritual essence and promise?

Mt. Contradiction*—target practice in the Alps,* above Andermatt. The disappearing glacier in the background was once of the first to be covered with reflective foil in an effort to "combat" the self-evident effects of dramatic Climate Change.

Urnerland, *center & heart of the Alps . . .*

Muted Snake—behind
Brownlee Dam . . . present
Idaho & Oregon border

NO
PROJECT
BY SURV
CA

ICE
NITORED
LLANCE
RA

About Cliff Crego . . .

Cliff Crego is a composer, (former) conductor, teacher, poet, translator, and art / nature photographer.

All black & white photographs (except TRINITY TEST), and all essays & miniatures included in this small collection, are his own.

He is currently on an extended bike / ski / mountaineering trek of the Pacific Northwest. As a matter of principle, he does not use vehicles of any kind powered by fossil fuels.

His base in North America is in the rugged and beautiful Wallowas, in an isolated corner of northeast Oregon;
In Europe, he is based both in the Netherlands, and the central part of the German-speaking Swiss Alps.

Weekly updates of his photos, poems & metaphysical journals for this trip and other fieldwork can be viewed at:

www.picture-poems.com

Pinkfaries *(Clarkia pulchella),* named for William Clark of the Corps of Discovery, first seen by Europeans in 1805 on the Clearwater River, near Kooskia, *ID*

"During times of universal deceit, telling the truth becomes a revolutionary act."

George Orwell

Please send comments or recommendations
to **cliff@picture-poems.com**

It may soon be possible to have an entire collection of documentaries like the one outlined above streamed and freely available online. If you have ideas concerning how to make this possible, please feel free to contact me directly.

That might make for a different world, indeed!

www.ingramcontent.com/pod-product-compliance
Ingram Content Group UK Ltd.
Pitfield, Milton Keynes, MK11 3LW, UK
UKHW021050270726
13967UKWH00012B/116

9 780557 949953